CATTLE AND OIL

The Growth of Texas Industries

Trisha James

NEW YORK

Published in 2010 by The Rosen Publishing Group, Inc.
29 East 21st Street, New York, NY 10010

Book Design: Haley W. Harasymiw

Photo Credits: Cover and interior borders and backgrounds, pp. 5–9, 15, 16, 28, 29 Shutterstock.com;
pp. 10, 14 Wikimedia Commons; p. 11 © Geoff Brightling/Getty Images; p. 12 © Popperfoto/Getty Images;
p. 17 © Getty Images; pp. 18, 22–25 © Hulton Archive/Getty Images; p. 20 © Getty Images News; pp. 26–27
© Time & Life Pictures/Getty Images.

Library of Congress Cataloging-in-Publication Data

James, Trisha.
 Cattle and oil : the growth of Texas industries / Trisha James.
     p. cm. -- (Spotlight on Texas)
 Includes index.
 ISBN 978-1-61532-475-0 (pbk.)
 6-pack ISBN: 978-1-61532-476-7
 ISBN 978-1-61532-477-4 (library binding)
 1. Texas--History--Juvenile literature. 2. Texas--Economic conditions--Juvenile literature. 3. Industries--Texas-
-History--Juvenile literature. I. Title.
 F386.3.J36 2010
 976.4--dc22
                                         2009031347

Manufactured in the United States of America

CPSIA Compliance Information: Batch # WW1ORC: For further information contact Rosen Publishing, New York, New York at 1-800-237-9932.

CONTENTS

LAND OF MANY INDUSTRIES

When many people think of Texas, they think of cattle and oil. The growth of these industries, or businesses, helped increase the state's wealth and population. The more successful these industries were, the more successful Texas was.

Today's Texas **economy** depends on industries such as **technology**, banking, and health care. However, these businesses might never have begun without cattle and oil. Perhaps the first settlers wouldn't have built communities in Texas without them. It's possible the history of Texas would have been completely different!

In this book, we'll look at the history of Texas cattle and oil industries and learn how they shaped the history of the state. We'll also look at some other Texas industries.

United States

TEXAS
Houston

Most Texans today live in and around cities such as Houston, shown above.

Early Texas Farmers

Perhaps as long as 37,000 years ago, the **ancestors** of modern Native Americans arrived in Texas. They found a land full of **natural resources**. Most Texas tribes traveled around and hunted wild animals, such as buffalo, deer, rabbits, and lizards. They gathered roots and fruits as well.

Parts of Texas had good farmland. The people there built homes. They planted foods such as corn, beans, squash, tomatoes, peanuts, and potatoes. Some raised cotton to make cloth as well.

Spanish **explorers** arrived in the early 1500s. Spanish settlers brought new crops, such as wheat, oats, onions, and peas. They also brought animals, such as horses, hogs, and cattle. **Livestock** fed on the wild grasses that covered about two-thirds of Texas. Farming became a way of life. A steady source of food made it possible to settle in one place.

Cotton is still the most successful crop in Texas. This picture shows a modern cotton field.

Texas under Spanish rule had small farms at first. Although Spain claimed the land, Native Americans occupied most of it. However, Mexico won independence from Spain in 1821. The Mexican government wanted greater control of Texas. To accomplish that, more settlers were needed. The government invited U.S. settlers into the area.

Stephen Austin had a land grant first given to his father, Moses. He brought about 300 families to Texas. Settlers received land for animals to **graze** on and land to plant crops. Many settlers found they could make a lot of money raising and selling cattle.

Texas longhorn

In 1836, Texas won its independence from Mexico. In 1845, it became part of the United States. A time of great growth for the cattle industry began.

Texas longhorns can live in hot weather without much water. They eat weeds, cactus, and brush.

RANCHES IN THE 1800s

Farms that raise livestock are called ranches. In the 1800s, the wide plains of Texas were ideal for open-range grazing. This meant cattle weren't fenced in. They could wander wherever they wanted and eat whatever grasses they found.

Certain events happened every year on ranches. Cattle gave birth to calves in the spring. Ranchers set them loose to live and eat on the range. In the fall, they were rounded up. Some cattle were taken to markets to be sold. Others were kept to have calves in the spring. Then the events began again.

For most of the 1800s, Texas didn't have railroads to carry the cattle to markets. Instead, they were "driven" to markets that were sometimes far away. A cattle drive is the controlled movement of a large number of cattle from one place to another. Ranches often hired cowboys to drive cattle.

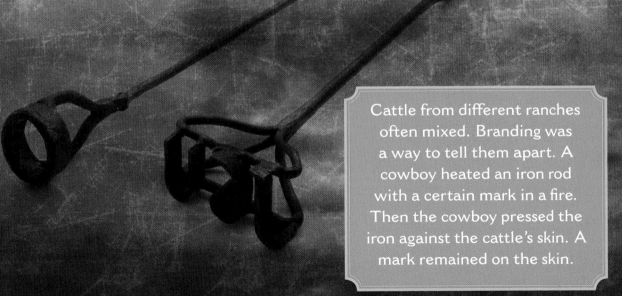

Cattle from different ranches often mixed. Branding was a way to tell them apart. A cowboy heated an iron rod with a certain mark in a fire. Then the cowboy pressed the iron against the cattle's skin. A mark remained on the skin.

Cattle drives weren't easy. Cowboys had to ride through bad weather, sleep outside, and eat little for weeks. They traveled on horseback on all sides of the herd to keep them moving in the right direction. Some drives were made up of 2,500 cows!

Cattle trails were "roads" taken by cowboys and their cattle. Many herds followed trails from Texas to Louisiana, Missouri, Arkansas, and Mississippi. Some cattle drives even went to California! Cattle were driven wherever there were people who wanted meat.

In the mid-1800s, railroad lines spread across the United States. Ranchers drove cattle to the closest railroad station. The cattle were loaded into cars and taken to markets. As railroads moved into Texas in the late 1800s, long cattle drives happened less often.

This map shows some famous cattle trails. The land north of Texas was called Indian Territory. Native Americans often allowed cattle herds to pass through peacefully for a price.

COW ★ TOWNS

Texas became more populated as the cattle industry grew. Communities called cow towns grew up along the cattle trails. Cowboys needed places to rest, eat, and have fun after months of hard, lonely work.

Cow towns became known for their lawlessness. Many stories of famous cowboys began in cow towns. Some cow towns were Abilene, Wichita, and Dodge City, Kansas; Abilene, Amarillo, Fort Worth, and Wichita Falls, Texas; and Cheyenne, Wyoming.

Bose Ikard

Bose Ikard was born a slave in Mississippi in 1843. When he was young, he moved with his owner to a ranch in Texas. Ikard learned to ride horses and rope cattle. He later got his freedom. Ikard then worked for ranchers Oliver Loving and Charles Goodnight. He drove cattle on the Goodnight-Loving Trail. Goodnight said Ikard was one of the best cowboys he ever had and a good friend. Ikard died in 1929 at the age of 85.

Wichita Falls was home first to Native Americans and then to cattle ranchers in the 1860s. A railroad was built through it in 1882. You can see the trains in the picture.

Today's Ranches

By the end of the 1800s, the cattle industry was changing. Open-range grazing gradually ended. Ranchers bought land so their own cattle had enough water and grass. They fenced off their land using twisted wire with sharp points called barbed wire. Cattlemen without land found themselves in trouble during very dry weather in the 1880s. "Fence wars" began with landless ranchers cutting wire fences to let their cattle onto others' land. By the end of the century, only cattle ranchers with land could stay in business.

Most cattle ranches in Texas today are feedlots. On feedlots, cattle are given corn and grains to eat. More cattle can be raised in less space than needed on open ranges. Other modern ranching tools include computers, electric branding irons, and helicopters!

barbed wire

Texas Fever

The Texas cattle industry took a great blow in the late 1800s. Some cattle got an illness that would become known as "Texas fever." As cattle were driven across the open range, they spread the deadly illness to other cows. In 1885, Kansas banned Texas cattle within its borders.

By the mid-1980s, Texas had more cattle on feedlots than any other state. Feedlots helped the growth of the corn industry in Texas, too.

Discovering Oil

Oil is another major part of the Texas economy. Oil industry roots go further back in history than the cattle industry. In July 1543, Spanish explorers traveling with Hernando De Soto saw oil floating on Galveston Bay. One of them, Luis de Moscoso Alvarado, wrote that they used this thick oil to fill cracks in their ships.

The oil the explorers found is called crude oil or petroleum (puh-TROH-lee-uhm). It's a natural resource called a **fossil fuel**. Found deep within rock, crude oil is **refined** to become fuels we can use. In the mid-1800s, it was made into a fuel called kerosene (KEHR-uh-seen). Kerosene creates light when burned. After the American Civil War ended in 1865, the United States began to use oil products as fuel. These took the place of steam and coal.

Oil in Other Parts of the United States

In the early 1800s, the area around Titusville, Pennsylvania, was known to have oil. Some had made its way to the surface. People used it as a drug to treat illnesses! At first, no one knew how to reach the oil below the surface. In the 1850s, the Seneca Oil Company sent Edwin Drake to drill near Titusville. He hired Billy Smith and his two sons. The men struck oil in 1859. The U.S. oil industry had begun.

Although more oil would be found in Texas, the industry began in Pennsylvania. Edwin Drake is shown here in a top hat. The Smiths are shown near their oil well.

THE OIL BOOM

In 1894, the first major oil business in Texas began near Corsicana in Navarro County. The area was known as the Corsicana oil field. It proved Texas had oil in great amounts. Joseph S. Cullinan set up the first Texas **refinery** there in 1898. However, it wasn't until January 10, 1901, that the oil business began to boom.

Near Beaumont, Texas, oil **prospector** Anthony F. Lucas drilled a well about 1,100 feet (335 m) deep. Oil shot more than 100 feet (30 m) into the air. The well filled about 900,000 barrels in just 9 days! By 1902, Spindletop oil field was producing about 17.5 million barrels a year. This was more than all other U.S. oil fields combined!

How Oil Forms

1. Millions of years ago, plants and animals die in a body of water.

2. The dead matter sinks and is quickly covered by mud and other matter on the sea floor.

3. More layers of sand and mud cover the first layer.

4. The weight of the layers presses them together and creates heat.

5. The matter changes into oil.

6. The oil leaks into spaces within rocks and remains there.

This picture shows oil gushing out of the oil well at Spindletop oil field in 1901.

Many oil companies began during the 1900s. Some still exist today. A lot of oil was being produced, so prices dropped very low. At one time, oil could be bought for three cents a barrel. That was less than the cost of water!

Much like the California gold rush of the 1840s, people flocked to Texas to find oil. Beaumont's population went from about 10,000 to 50,000 in just a few years. A town that grows very quickly is called a boomtown. Boomtowns were also called ragtowns and tent cities because of their poor housing. They were filled with people who hoped to find oil or to sell supplies to those looking for oil.

Texas oil field in 1901

When the eastern Texas oil fields opened in the 1930s, the Texas economy had greatly changed. An agricultural economy had become an oil economy.

People who drilled oil wells where oil wasn't known to exist were called wildcatters. Many lived in boomtowns such as this one.

OIL CHANGES LIVES

The huge supply of oil changed Texas and the United States in a short amount of time. Trains and ships changed from steam and coal power to oil power. Cars and planes were new inventions in the early 1900s. Motor oil and gasoline, made from crude oil, became important fuels for them, too.

On farms, new oil-powered machines such as tractors helped farmers raise and gather crops with less time and effort. In many homes, oil was used for heat. Factory machines ran on oil as well. People left farm work for factory work. By 1950, more Texans were living in cities than ever before.

Oil helped Texas become a rich state. The state government began taxing oil producers in 1905. The state used tax money for its schools and public buildings and programs.

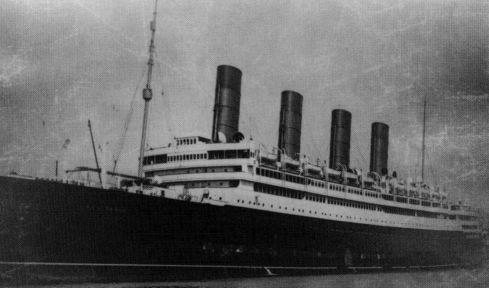

Shown at left is the first oil-burning train of the Great Western Railway. Above is a ship that was changed from coal power to oil power.

In 1931, the U.S. government decided to limit the amount of oil that could be produced. This would keep the price from dropping too low. It would also make sure that the oil didn't run out. Oil began to arrive from other countries, so Texas oil wasn't needed. However, Texas refineries kept busy refining crude oil from countries such as Saudi Arabia, Canada, and Mexico.

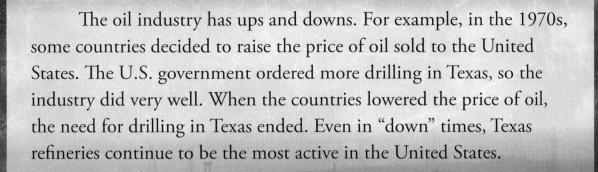

The oil industry has ups and downs. For example, in the 1970s, some countries decided to raise the price of oil sold to the United States. The U.S. government ordered more drilling in Texas, so the industry did very well. When the countries lowered the price of oil, the need for drilling in Texas ended. Even in "down" times, Texas refineries continue to be the most active in the United States.

Offshore drilling around Texas increased in the 1970s, especially in Galveston Bay. Goods made from oil, such as a kind of rubber, continue to keep the industry active.

More Texas Industries

Besides oil and cattle, Texas leads other U.S. industries. **Natural gas** is a fossil fuel often found with crude oil. The rise of the oil industry led to the success of the natural gas industry.

Texas is also a center of technology. For example, **NASA**'s Lyndon B. Johnson Space Center is located in Houston. All U.S. flights into space are controlled from there. In addition, many computer companies are based in Texas.

A model of a space shuttle at the Houston Space Center

Texas is a top producer of U.S. wind energy. A kind of windmill called a turbine has blades that turn in the wind. This movement creates electricity without producing waste that harms Earth. Many people hope to use more wind energy in the future. Wind energy will continue to be one of many important Texas industries.

A wind farm is an area with many wind turbines. The land between turbines can be used for planting crops or for other purposes.

READER RESPONSE PROJECTS

- Choose an industry in the chapter "More Texas Industries." Using the Internet and library, find out how this industry started in Texas and how it grew. Use your notes to create a short book. Include pictures to help tell your story.

- Many people became rich through the Texas oil boom, including Ima Hogg, J. G. Hardin, Ruth Legett Jones, and Don and Sybil Harrington. Use the Internet or library to read about someone who used their oil money to help others. Create a poster showing how this person changed Texas.

- Use your library or the Internet to read more about Texas cowboys and cowgirls. Find out about their daily lives. Create a project that teaches others about cowboy life. Show your class how to make a cowboy food, sing a cowboy song, or complete another project about cowboys.

GLOSSARY

ancestor (AN-sehs-tuhr) A person in your family who lived long ago.

economy (ih-KAH-nuh-mee) The way a country or business manages its supplies, power, and money.

explorer (ihk-SPLOHR-uhr) One who travels to find new lands.

fossil fuel (FAH-suhl FYOOL) A fuel, such as coal or natural gas, made from plants and animals that died millions of years ago.

graze (GRAYZ) To feed on grass.

livestock (LYV-stahk) Animals raised for food or other products.

NASA (NAA-suh) National Aeronautics and Space Administration, the United States' space office.

natural gas (NA-chuh-ruhl GAS) A mix of gases found deep within Earth that can be used as fuel.

natural resource (NA-chuh-ruhl REE-sohrs) Something in nature that can be used by people.

prospector (PRAH-spehk-tuhr) A person who travels around an area looking for a natural resource.

refine (rih-FYN) To make into a more pure and usable form.

refinery (rih-FY-nuh-ree) A place where something is refined.

technology (tehk-NAH-luh-jee) Industry that deals with electronics.

INDEX

Due to the changing nature of Internet links, the Rosen Publishing Group, Inc., has developed an online list of Web sites related to the subject of this book. This site is updated regularly. Please use this link to access the list: **http://www.rcbmlinks.com/sot/catoil/**